Real Estate Investor:

How To Make Six Figures By Buying, Renovating and Flipping Properties in 2017

JESSICA FRIEDMAN

Copyright 2014 by Jessica Friedman - All rights reserved.

This document is geared towards providing exact and reliable information in regards to the topic and issue covered. The publication is sold with the idea that the publisher is not required to render accounting, officially permitted, or otherwise, qualified services. If advice is necessary, legal or professional, a practiced individual in the profession should be ordered.

- From a Declaration of Principles which was accepted and approved equally by a Committee of the American Bar Association and a Committee of Publishers and Associations.

In no way is it legal to reproduce, duplicate, or transmit any part of this document in either electronic means or in printed format. Recording of this publication is strictly prohibited and any storage of this document is not allowed unless with written permission from the publisher. All rights reserved.

The information provided herein is stated to be truthful and consistent, in that any liability, in terms of inattention or otherwise, by any usage or abuse of any policies, processes, or directions contained within is the solitary and utter responsibility of the recipient reader. Under no circumstances will any legal responsibility or blame be held against the publisher for any reparation, damages, or monetary loss due to the information herein, either directly or indirectly.

Respective authors own all copyrights not held by the publisher.

The information herein is offered for informational purposes solely, and is universal as so. The presentation of the information is without contract or any type of guarantee assurance.

The trademarks that are used are without any consent, and the publication of the trademark is without permission or backing by the trademark owner. All trademarks and brands within this book are for clarifying purposes only and are the owned by the owners themselves, not affiliated with this document.

Table of Contents

Introduction 5

Chapter 1 – Learning the Value of Location 6

Chapter 2 – Flipping Homes as a Business 9

Chapter 3 – Anticipating Cost and Profits 17

Chapter 4 – Pick a Market to Master 21

Chapter 5 – Places to Avoid 24

Chapter 6 – The Pre-buying Process 27

Chapter 7 – Reasons Why Properties Are Sold Cheap 31

Chapter 8 – Funding Your Business 33

Chapter 9 – Negotiating for the Property 39

Chapter 10 – Getting Things Fixed 43

Chapter 11 – Selling the Property 49

Chapter 12 – Earning 6-figures from Your Real Estate Business 54

Conclusion 58

Introduction

I want to thank you and congratulate you for downloading the book, *"Real Estate Investor"*.

This book contains proven steps and strategies on how to start a house flipping business.

Most beginners in house flipping only know about this industry through the TV shows about it. In these TV shows, we see contractors and even celebrities try to make money by renovating old houses. The shows however, present more of the drama rather than the business behind the industry.

In this book, we will try to discuss the business side of the process. We will talk about how you can start by buying the first property that you are going to flip. We will also talk about the people that you need to work with and the best practices when dealing with both buyers and sellers.

To succeed in this business, and start earning a six-figure income, you need to know how to take calculated risks. You should also know how to walk away from bad deals. This book will teach you how to do both of these.

Thanks again for downloading this book, I hope you enjoy it!

Chapter 1 – Learning the Value of Location

The real estate market refers to the industry of buyers and sellers of real property. When buyers and sellers meet and agree on a price, they end up making a transaction. In its simplest form, a real estate transaction involves a buyer obtaining property from the seller at an agreed upon price.

With markets these days however, nothing seems simple. As with other types of investments, investing in real estate also includes other players. This includes the government which sets up policies for the entire market to follow. We also have the brokers whose main purpose is to facilitate the transactions and make everything go smoothly for both buyers and sellers.

Most importantly, you also need to consider the important market factors. These are the events in the market that lead to price changes. A number of factors can affect the price of the property. We will discuss these factors in this chapter.

Location

There is a saying among real estate business people:

"In real estate, there are three important factors to consider; location, location, location."

Even with all the technological advances today for marketing properties and reaching out to new market, this rule still hasn't changed. If you are in the housing business, location is still the single most important factor to consider. The location of a property directly determines its price.

A house in a suburban area an hour away from the city will be more expensive than a house with the same design three hours away. The only way for the house farther from the city to increase its value is if an establishment with good location value, like a hospital, school, mall or an important government office, opens near it.

You should consider this when you are starting out in the house flipping business. It will be much easier to sell a house if it is in a prime location. Now, let's look into what makes a prime location in the housing market.

Good schools

Good schools are always a priority for families moving into a new city. Most people want high quality schools to be near their home so that the parents could just drop off the kids before work. This also means that the parents will be able to go to the after-work school shows of the children.

In the next chapters, you will need to pick a part of your city where you will focus you house flipping operations. You should consider these factors if you want to sell your properties fast after renovations.

Convenient nearby establishments

You should also consider the establishments around the area of the properties you buy. Other convenience establishments include hospitals, grocery stores and even malls. You should consider how long it will take to go to these establishments from the property. Your future buyers will consider this when thinking of buying the property. You should consider it too.

The reputation of the neighborhood

You will also learn that people always consider the reputation of the neighborhood when looking for a home. Most people just want somewhere safe where they can raise their children in. If you are choosing an area in your city to start buying and selling houses, choose to buy from great neighborhoods first. The worst house in a good neighborhood will always sell faster than the best

Real Estate Investor

house in a bad one.

Chapter 2 – Flipping Homes as a Business

Now that you are familiar with the concept of buying and selling real properties, let's discuss the specific business of flipping homes.

Flipping refers to renovating homes and other types of real property for profit. In this business, you will need to buy a home that is already established. Ideally, you need to get the home at a low price (lower than the average selling price in the local market). The lower the price of the home that you get, the higher the potential income will be.

After buying your first property, you will need to start designing the home. The goal is to repair it, make it more presentable and add features to it. All the changes that you make will cost money. The goal of these changes is to increase the value of the property. This is the tricky part of the business. You will need to learn about the features that people want to see in their homes. You need to learn the home features that people are willing to pay extra for.

In this chapter, we will discuss how you should start with your home flipping business.

Avoid starting in an economic bubble

Investing in real property is risky business if you do not know what you are doing. Most people already know the process of buying, renovating and selling homes. If you take this process for granted when you start however, you may be surprised about how stressful the whole project can be. To make sure that you have the proper expectations coming in, you should ask for advice from people who are already in the business.

Real Estate Investor

When asking for advice, you need to ask about the current status of the market. Your biggest concern is entering the market in an economic bubble.

An economic bubble is a term used by economists when the prices in the market are generally inflated, compared to their true market value or the intrinsic values of the properties listed. In other words, in a bubble, homes are extremely expensive. A bubble can lead to big profits if you are already selling your property. If you are just buying your first set of properties to flip however, you best wait until the bubble is over.

A real estate bubble can happen because of different reasons. Let's say you live in a small town. In an area nearby, three big companies opened factories, providing high paying jobs to people. These companies will add more occupants to surrounding towns. Since your town is the closest, people working in the new factories check your suburban areas for a new home. Buyers are flocking in to buy properties. The increase in demand increases the asking prices for properties.

This is an example of how demand increases the prices of properties in a specific area. The hype and increased prices do not always lead into a bubble. Usually, there are unforeseen factors that would create the bubble. Buying in credit is one example of such a factor. When people invest using credit, bad things usually happen. Prices usually increase but not because of an increase in demand or a decrease in supply.

Demand refers to the number or market participants who are willing and able to make a transaction. When people buy using credit, more market participants think that they have the capacity to buy. This artificially increases the demand, which in turn leads to an increase in price.

The increase in demand also pushes more real estate owners to sell their own properties to make profit. Properties that were difficult to sell, are now selling for three times the prices.

Real Estate Investor

There are two types of buyers in the real estate market. The first one is the genuine buyer. This type of buyer intends to buy property to actually use it. The second type is the investor. The investor has money to spare and is willing to take the risk of buying a property, hoping that it will increase in value over time. When they are satisfied with the value of the property, they can sell it for a profit.

When there is hype in the market, the number of investor buyers in an area tends to increase. In part, they are also responsible for the increase of prices of the properties in a certain area.

The market tends to correct itself when there is a discrepancy. Let's say a local bank provided the credit that the real estate investors used to invest in your town. However, news came out that the factories backed out of the deal. They will no longer continue to build a factory near your town.

This will affect the market as well. Suddenly, there is a high number of properties for sale in the market but the number of buyers drastically decreased. Investors desperately sell of the properties that they still have on hand. The decrease in demand and increase in supply of properties in the market will lead to a dip in the prices.

If you are not participating in the real estate market, you will barely notice these factors. They have little effect on your own life. If you happen to buy a property at the time of the bubble however, you may be in big trouble.

When the bubble burst, investors who entered the market late are usually at a losing position. They bought the property when prices were high. Not only are they unable to make a profit, but they are also likely to lose money if they sell the property right away. If they do decide to hold on to the property until the market recovers, they end up freezing their capital on an investment that is not increasing in value.

This is the scenario that you want to avoid when you are starting in the business.

Pair up with the right professionals

If you are sure that the demand in the market is genuine and there is no economic bubble, you can now start with buying your first property. The first step in doing this is by looking for a real estate broker. Real estate brokers are professionals who keep a list of properties to sell. When you are new in the business, you usually do not have a lot of connections yet to point you in the right direction for the best properties in the area. Your broker will help you in building these connections and looking for properties that fit your preference.

Brokers love making deals with investors because these types of buyers usually keep coming back to the market to buy and sell properties. The broker makes money for each property he or she buys and sells.

Aside from brokers, you also need to work with structural engineers. Most of the properties that you will be renovating are more than a decade old. You need to make sure that these properties are still structurally sound for the next occupant. If the foundation of the property has a big damage, you may end up spending a fortune to have it repaired. This may cancel out any profit that you can gain from the property.

You will also need to work with an interior designer and a supplier of construction and renovations supplies. Even if you have a good eye for design, a designer will be helpful in providing advice on how to apply your ideas when doing the renovations. They may also have their own input on how to achieve certain themes in your design.

You will also need to work with contractors, depending on the type of renovation that the property requires. A big renovation project will require a lot of man hours. If you only work by yourself, it will take long before you can sell the house. Working with contract workers to help you achieve your vision will allow you to meet deadlines and sell the house faster. The faster the work is done, the lower the cost.

Become a master of your business area

Your mastery of an area when buying and selling is your best asset when buying properties. With this in mind, you should master the different locations in the city or town where you wish to operate. Start by identifying the areas where you want to buy and sell properties.

In a major city, you will be able to see a lot of suburban neighborhoods. If you are planning to flip these types of home, you should look into the good and bad sides of these neighborhoods. One neighborhood, for instance, may have worse traffic than the others. A neighborhood by the river may have a great view of the natural scenery.

You should familiarize yourself with these factors before you start buying properties.

If you are operating in New York City for instance, you should make sure that you are aware of all the streets, neighborhoods and communities in your city. Each part of the city has its own value. In the beginning, you want to read up on all the news about the areas in the city where properties are selling fast. More importantly, you should look into news and gossip on the next big places in the city. These are the places where you want to buy properties from.

Buying based on the chatter in the market can be risky. If the information that you base your decision to make a purchase on is incorrect, you may end up unable to sell the property. You should fact check all the information that you are getting. If there is no evidence to support a rumor, do not pull the trigger.

Learn the going prices of properties in the area

Brokers usually have access to a list of the prices of recently bought and sold properties. You want to keep track of these prices before you actually start buying properties. By looking at the 'comps' you will be able to check the limit of the market. Buyers usually set a budget when buying property. Some of them may buy properties slightly over the budget; however, they still have a limit. By checking the comps of properties in the area, you will be able to know the selling prices of the properties. With knowledge of the prices of past transactions in the area, you will be able to decide on your own buying price when choosing a property.

Beginner's Tip:

Do not rely on listing prices when making your research. Most listing prices are inflated because the sellers are making room for haggling. The prices generally go down to a selling price 5%-20% of the listed prices.

Decide on the type of property that you want to flip

You will also need to consider the type of property that you want to work on. Your options will also depend on the types of properties available in your area. If you are in a city for example, you may see that the only available properties for renovating are condominium units and apartments. If you are have a suburban area near you, you may also have the option to renovate homes.

Aside from these basic housing properties, you may also have the option to renovate luxury properties. These include rest houses and vacation homes. This may be available in your area if you have relaxing geographical features nearby like rivers, lakes, the ocean or mountains.

In the beginning, it is wise to stick only to renovating one type of property. Ideally, you should stick to a property type that you are already familiar with. The best way to look at the type of property that you want to work on is by visiting other properties for sale in your area. For instance, you can start by looking into the houses sold in the local neighborhood.

When checking these properties, you should check both poorly maintained properties and the ones that are fully renovated. This way, you will be able to compare the different conditions of properties in the market. You will also be able to compare prices based on their different conditions.

Beginner tips:

Beginners often make the mistake of biting off more than they can chew. People coming into this business usually have a vision in mind with each house they see. Sometimes, these visions are not very practical from a business standpoint. Most creative types who go into this business often want to work with big houses with big renovations. Most of the time, beginners take houses that take long to renovate. Others also choose to add features that do not add a lot of value to the home.

To avoid this mistake, you should start small with your flipping business. Instead of breaking the bank with your first purchase, try to minimize the expenses. You can do this by buying 'entry level homes'. These are homes that are priced below the average price of the houses currently listed on the market. If the average home in the suburbs of the city for example, sells for $250,000, you want to get a house that sells between $80,000 and $150,000. Your goal when flipping is to make that property a $250,000- $300,000 house.

In a listing, you will often see that price tags vary, according to the houses' location and their size. In terms of location, houses are usually higher priced if they are near other important places. For instance, a home near a hospital will be much more expensive compared to a home that is in the outskirts of town. For now, focus on getting a property in a location that easily sells. Get the

Real Estate Investor

average price of the sold properties in that area from your broker and decide on the entry price that you will commit to your first property.

Chapter 3 – Anticipating Cost and Profits

The home flipping business can be expensive. First, you will need to have the money to buy the home. Even if you buy it using a loan, you will still need to use cash in the beginning for down payments and the legal fees that may come with the purchase.

After paying the cost of the house, you will also need to pay for the renovations. This includes the salary of the people working for you and the cost of the materials used in the renovation. Beginner house flippers take these amounts from their own pockets, assuming that they will regain all the money back and make profits when they do sell the house.

Not all of them however, actually do make a profit. Some of them even get several losing ventures in a row. Most of these people failed to anticipate the actual cost that they would spend on the home. Some of them spent too much on the house or in the renovations. Others hold on to the property too long, increasing their interest rates. In general, they all failed to anticipate the true cost of the project.

Treat each property as an independent project

Buying and selling a property must be treated like a project. By this, we mean that it should be short term and it should have a definite start and end date. In between these dates, you must have clearly defined tasks that will lead to the completion of the project. Each task will cost you money, so you want to make sure that they are all done on time.

Having this mindset coming in will allow you to organize all the tasks that need to be done before the house could be sold. As the person with the most to gain for this project, you should manage it to make sure that everything is done right.

Consider all the extra expenses when calculating the cost

Try to take all expected costs into consideration when you are making your calculations. Make sure that you consider the commission rate of the broker. They are your primary agent for selling. They also gain if you sell are able to the house fast. You can motivate your brokers to sell faster if you give them better commissions than the ones in their other property.

Depending on your arrangement with your broker, you should also consider the cost of marketing the property. You will need to list the property for sale where it will get the best coverage. Most of the time, the brokers will do this for you when you are ready to sell. However, it may lead to more expenses for both of you.

Anticipating profits

When you calculate the profits that you can make, consider the lowest and highest prices in the comps that your broker gives you. These prices will serve as a guide on how much you may gain if you finish the project soon.

Ideally, the total cost of the house and the cost of renovation should be 50% of the highest selling price of the houses sold recently in the area. This will give you a lot of wiggle room when you are selling. If the cost of the property is near 75-80% of the anticipated selling price, you should start to worry because your profits are dwindling away.

Managing your income

The money that you take in from your project should be divided up. First, you will need to make sure that all outstanding expenses are paid off fast. These include commissions and salaries of the people you work with. Freelance workers appreciate an employer who pays the right amount and on time. They are more likely to work with you and encourage other people do so as well if you have no issues with distributing money.

Second, you will also need to consider the capital of your business. The amount that covers the capital should be returned back to your business. By returning this amount back to your business, you will be able to buy and flip more properties in the future. This will ensure the survival of your business.

After covering all the cost of the business, you are left with the net income or the profits. Most people would put this amount back to their personal funds, as a reward for their hard work. Some spend it freely as a way for them to reward themselves for their effort.

A wiser person, though would take part of the net profits and use it as an insurance. This amount would go to a savings account separate from your personal account. It should be used when you plan to expand your business or when you get a business emergency. Ideally, you want this spent on the growth of your business. By saving part of your profits, you will be able to afford to flip bigger properties in the future.

There will be times when the business will need some extra cash to weather the tough times. You could also use this amount. Saving part of the profit will keep you motivated to sell properties fast during the good times. The amount that you save will allow you to slow down during the lean months or years. In some stretches, there may not be a lot of properties available on the market. This usually happens when an area is saturated with real estate investors. When this happens to your area of operation, you should consider moving to another location to increase the chances of finding a good home to flip. The time when you are looking for a property also costs you money. At this point, you are spending time while you still do not have an anticipated return for your efforts.

Your saved amount could also be used in times of recession. At this time, the prices of the properties you own tend to go down. This means that you will not be able to sell your properties at the anticipated prices. Because most people in the economy took a financial hit, it may also take some time for you to sell your properties. Your savings could be used for living expenses while the recession is ongoing. By having an amount saved for this kind of economic environment, you will be able to keep doing business and make the logical business decisions even when you are not gaining profits.

If you want to last long in this business, you need to manage your money well.

Chapter 4 – Pick a Market to Master

The real estate world can also be subdivided into different submarkets. In the big cities, you have apartments and condominium units. In the rural areas, you have farming properties and sources of industrial materials. Each of these types of properties has their own target market to cater to.

In the house-flipping business, you cater to the people who need new homes. These are the end buyers of your product. To know what type of people you are selling to, visit your friends who own properties similar to the one that you are selling. You want to make a profile of the people who are more likely to be able to afford the houses at the prices you are willing to sell them.

To succeed in this business, you need to learn all about your market. Here are some of the questions that you need to answer while you are doing research:

What is the size of their family?

The size of the family is one of the biggest factors that home buyers consider. If they had a choice, they would want a room for every member of the family. You best consider the average family size of the people living in the areas where you operate. If you are selling a 4-bedroom suburban home for instance, you will be wasting your time selling to a single male. You are more likely to close the deal with a married couple with one or two kids.

How much is their average budget for buying properties?

Most of the time, buyers already have a budget coming into the market. People always lean on the more conservative side when choosing a budget. Most of the properties in the market will be priced beyond their budgets. Because of this, they will be forced to adjust their budget so that it meets the prices in the market.

When you are doing your research, you should already find out the average amount that people would set as their initial budget for buying a home. In the beginning, while you are still starting out, you want to sell properties fast. To achieve this, you will need to make sure that the prices of the properties you are selling are as near the average budget amount as possible.

This way, people will consider your property first when they are looking for homes in the market.

What needs do they want to meet for buying a new home?

People will often consider paying a premium price for a property if it meets the need that they want to satisfy. One of the most common reasons for moving to a new home is an increase in the size of the family. A family with two boys for instance, may share a bedroom when they are young. As they grow older however, the parents may want a separate room for each. When you consider the design of the home, you should also consider these factors. You will be able to sell homes faster when the property you sell meets the needs of the general market.

What types of homes do jobs in your area are more likely to afford?

Another reason people have for buying a new home is relocating for a new job. If people regularly come to your city for work, you should consider the types of jobs of people who are more likely to buy homes in your neighborhood. Let's say you have a university near the property you are selling. You should check if the people who live in that area are predominantly students and faculty of the said school.

It this is the case, you will be able to adjust your renovations to meet the needs of these types of people. For instance, a teacher will need a space in the house for his or her own working area. Teachers generally, are more likely to bring their work home with them. You could set one room in the ground floor of the house specifically for this purpose.

If you can identify the types of jobs that usually bring new families into your area of operation, you will also be able to make an intelligent guess on where these people are coming from. If your state is more lenient with accepting immigrant families for instance, you may find that there is an untapped market of home buyers from a specific country. You should consider designing and selling homes to the right market.

Lastly, you should think of your own questions that you want to find out about your target market.

Chapter 5 – Places to Avoid

When you are in the house flipping business, your first priority is to buy a home at a low price. With this mindset however, it is easy to fall into traps that may ensnare your budget for a long time. This may happen when you buy a property that is not ideal for flipping. In this chapter, we will discuss the types that you should avoid when making your first purchase.

1. Homes in flooded areas

Places that were struck by a natural calamity usually have low listings. However, there is a good reason why the prices are low: nobody wants to buy them. If you want to make your first flip fast, you should avoid these types of houses.

Places that flood often have geographical problems that are difficult to solve. For instance, the place may serve like a basin of water geographically. In this case, the geographical depression will always cause flooding.

Other frequently flooded areas are near a body of water that often overflows. A city near the ocean for example, is likely to become flooded every time a big storm comes inland.

There are possible solutions for properties in these types of areas. However, they usually take time to develop. Governments may build structures that lessen the impact of water like flood-control water ways, and dikes and seawalls. However, these projects take decades to complete.

If your area of business is generally prone to flooding, choose to buy in the parts of town that are least affected. These areas are usually in the higher parts of town. You may also choose to look for properties a few miles away from the nearest coastline or river. You will need extensive knowledge of the place or you to be able to get a good grasp of the extent of the flooding problems in an area. If you are new to the area, it is best to get the opinion of an expert of the areas that are usually heavily flooded. You can learn this by connecting with earth science professors and engineers in the local university.

2. Properties with heavy damage

Properties may also be priced low if it requires a lot of structural repairs. These types of properties are often too costly. You may want to avoid these types of flips in the beginning. The values of the properties you flip only increase when the renovations are actually done. These types of properties take a long time and a lot of capital to renovate. In general, you only want to buy a house that is structurally sound.

3. Homes with a past of violent crimes

When buying a home, you should look into its past owners. Try to look up the address on the internet. Your goal is to look for news reports about the place about violent crimes that happened in the neighborhood or even the exact house that you are planning to buy. Homebuyers nowadays are particular with these types of details. If a home is featured in the news for violent crimes, buyers will find it. This will give them a reason to either haggle for the property or turn it down altogether.

4. Extremely old homes

Old homes have their own market. However, buyers of these homes are usually focused on the historical value of a home rather than its true living condition. In addition, this market is usually too small to make a business of.

In general, you should avoid old homes as a beginner. Homes that were built back in the 30s and 40s, for instance may already have irreparable damages. Aside from foundational damage, the people who built these houses in the past may have been following a completely different set of regulations compared to what we have today. If you wish to bring this house into the market with the intention of selling it as a family home, you will need to make sure that any regulation neglected in the building of the house is complied with this time.

This may require you to make big changes in the house. In most cases, you may need to make sure that all the functional structures (piping, wiring and fixtures, foundation, wall materials) follow the current building code of your state.

The trick here is to find the sweet spot between older homes and newer ones. Generally, you want to get the newer ones on the market. However, you should consider that houses built within the decade tend to be difficult to haggle for. When looking for a property to flip, check the newer properties first. Only move to the older listings if you cannot get the newer homes for the price you want.

Chapter 6 – The Pre-buying Process

As stated in earlier chapters, you should consider each flip to be a short business project. The goal is to make as much money as you can fast. To learn if you will be able to accomplish these goals, you will need to do a short feasibility study. You should do this with every property that you are about to buy.

Go through the listing and visit all possible candidates

When looking through the local listing of properties, you should look for all the available information about the property before you even visit it. The first information you will see is the price. Right off the bat, you should already consider narrowing the options with the price. Aside from this, you could also narrow the selection by considering the location of the house. If it is frequently flooded, take it off your list.

Visit the homes

At this point, you should have the current listings of homes in your price range and in a good resell location. The next step is to go and visit the property. Ideally, you should have your engineer with you at this point. Generally, you want to check the integrity of the foundational structures of the house.

This is also a good time to have a firsthand experience of how the actual environment surrounding the house feels. At this point, you should make it a habit to make mental notes of the possible selling points of the house. You can go to the house during rush hour for example, to check how heavy the traffic is in the area. You could also visit the property when it is raining to check how flooded the roads are when it rains. Try to observe these little details because the future buyers of the property will notice them.

Identify the changes that will add value to the home

When visiting the home that you are considering to buy, you should already look into the areas that need improvement. You should put yourself in the buyer's shoes when looking for these flaws. Ask the seller's broker about the positive features of the house. They will be happy to enumerate them for you. Take note of these details so that you can use them when it is your time to sell. When listening to the broker trying to sell the property to you, also focus on the aspects that he may be leaving out. In each room being presented, take note of the parts that the broker fails to mention. Check them out yourself to see if there are damages or construction flaws that need to be fixed. If necessary, bring a notebook with you so that you will know what needs to be done.

Some fixes are obvious to spot. Mismatched tiles for instance tend to turn buyers off. The same goes for paint or wallpaper coming off the walls. These are the types of issues that you should be paying attention to in your first visit.

After visiting all the properties available in your area, make a list of the ones that you are planning to purchase. You may need to do a second visit of the property before you actually decide to close the deal.

On your second visit, you need to have your team with you. In this visit, your goal is to have the house checked for repairs needed that are not obvious in the first visit. This will include the wiring, the piping and the structural features of the house. At this point, you also need to go to the less visible areas of the house like the garage, basement and attic. You want to see if there are damages in these hidden areas.

While you are looking into these parts of the house, you should take note of the issues that you see and your ideas for fixing them. You should also include ideas that may come to your mind during these visits on how to upgrade the property.

Choose a property to make a deal with

After checking the properties, you will need to choose the one that you will work on. You and your broker will need to come up with an offer relative to the asking price of the property. By law, the broker is required to inform the owner of the property of all the offers made regardless of how low they are.

When coming up with an offer, first, you need to decide on your target price. Your target price will require you to consider the resell value of the property after you make all the necessary renovations. Let's say that the property is listed at $180,000. You and your engineers decided that the cost of the renovations and your ideas will be up to $50,000. However, after the renovations, your estimate selling price is only at $250,000. At this rate, you will only make $20,000 for all the risk you took and the effort you put in.

To increase the profits that you may get from your project, you will need to significantly lessen the buying price of the house. This job usually goes to your broker.

Your broker will probably tell you this but generally, the offer should be significantly lower than your target price so:

- **Review the work that needs to be done**

After deciding on the property to buy, take the time to sit down with your partners and the people who will be helping you with the project. You will need to present the plan for this project. State everything about the property and the changes that you want to make on it. After that, let the professionals offer their advice and possible solutions to the issues that you pointed out with the property. Lastly, you should present the limitations such as the timeline of the project and the budget limitations.

The point of this meeting is to make sure that everyone is on-board with the process. This will also confirm that the changes that you want for the project are doable, given the amount of time and the budget.

- **Calculate the After-Repair-Value**

Real Estate Investor

The biggest part of the meeting will be spend for you and your broker to agree on an after repair value. By confirming that the changes you want to make are doable, you will be able to decide on the selling price of the house. You will need to consider multiple factors to be able to arrive at this value. This includes the prices of similar houses in the area and the actual value added by your renovations. You will also need to consider factors like the cost of the materials and any appreciation in value for the time that lapsed since the renovation. Most fixes take only a few months, but if significant changes in the location happened in that time, the price of the property may be affected.

Chapter 7 – Reasons Why Properties Are Sold Cheap

The first step in buying a property is always to get it at a low price. Most people outside the real estate industry often think that it is impossible to consistently get properties below their market value. You'll be surprised how often this happens. By knowing the reasons why people sell properties undervalued, you will be able to know where to look and how to get properties with good price tags.

Here are some of the common reasons why properties are sold cheap:

Liquidation of assets

For most businesses, cash assets are always better than real property because of its liquidity. When a bank obtains a property for instance, they try to get rid of it as soon as possible by auctioning it off to the highest bigger. When you are looking for properties in the future, the foreclosed listings in the bank are some of the lowest priced properties you will find.

Aside from banks, there are instances when private individuals also want to liquidate their assets fast. A person leaving the country for good may want to wrap all legal and financial affairs before leaving. Because of the time factor, they may be forced to accept the highest offer for their property even if it is below the projected market value of the property.

Lack of knowledge about the property

It is also common for people to sell the property on their own without consulting professionals. Because of this, they often sell the property below its market value because of their lack of knowledge of the going rate of the properties around the area. Even if they did their research, they may fail to consider the future value of the property. Good brokers make it their business to know the things going on in their area of operation. They are well informed of the property deals being made in the background and the properties being planned in the future. This type of insider information is important if you want to succeed in the real estate business.

Speeding up the sale for legal reasons

When a property has more than one owner, it is sometimes necessary to sell the property fast to be able to give each person his or her share for that property. House owned by parents or close relatives often end up being sold fast by the heirs. None of them wants to maintain the property or to buy off the other heirs. In these cases, the best option is to sell the property fast to resolve the issue.

Homes stay too long in the market

In specific economic conditions, like right after a recession, you will find many cheap houses on the market. Because of the big supply, many of these homes stay long in the market. Some owners who are in need of the money or who are in a hurry to get rid of the property may end up accepting offers below the market values of their properties.

Poorly constructed or renovated homes

When a house is poorly constructed or maintained, it may not look appealing to most buyers. Because of the lack of offers for these properties, the sellers may decide to decrease the asking price for the property. Only when the property is below the market value will it start getting offers from buyers in the market. With some negotiations, the buyer may be able to push the price lower by citing the fixes that need to be done.

Chapter 8 – Funding Your Business

Now that you know the basic process before buying a home to flip, let's discuss how you are going to pay for the property. Most people are afraid to go into the house-flipping business because of the amount of money usually required for this type of business.

In this chapter, we will discuss the different ways to fund your business. Let's begin with the first one:

1. Using your own money

The easiest way to start with a house flipping business is by using your own money to purchase the property. Most sellers for properties will give you a discount if you can pay cash for the property. This gives them assurance that the deal will go through, compared to receiving check.

The downside of using your own money is that you are putting all the risk all into your own finances. Most beginners are not comfortable with that.

Many people using their own money to flip houses also get into the habit of spending more than they should. They go over the budget because no one is holding them accountable for the amount they are spending.

You must avoid this habit, especially if the renovations or upgrades that you are doing do not add much value to the after-repair value of the property.

One limitation for using your own money is that you will be limited on the scale of the project that you will take on. If your first few flips require easy fixes and upgrades for instance, you may want to take on another property. Sometimes, you have to pull the trigger and take one multiple properties even as a beginner. When a property with a good selling price relative to its retail value comes up in the market, you should always be ready to add it to your inventory.

When you are using only your own money, you will not be able to commit to a lot of properties. Most people will only be able to commit to a maximum or two or three properties. If you want to take advantage of good listings in the market, you should consider other means of funding.

2. Banking Loans

A banking loan is one of the first financing options to come to most people's minds when financing a house flipping business. The advantage of this type of financing scheme is that it is easy to find. You just need to go to the nearest bank that offers small business or even personal loans. You will need to fill up their forms and let them do their credit history check. After a few days, you will be contacted to see if your loan has been approved. Some will even have your loan approved in a day.

However, there are also some disadvantages with using this type of financing scheme. For instance, bank loans are dependent on the status of the economy. Usually, the interest rates are at their lowest right after a recession. At this point, the interest rates imposed by the Federal Bank (of the central bank of your country), is just above 0%. This happens when the Federal government is trying to boost the economy by lending money to banks and business. At this point, the banks also follow their lead and also lower their borrowing interest rates.

The downside is that most people are usually not in a buying mood for a house right after a recession. People who were hit by the recession may have seen their investment funds diminished.

As the economy improves, the Feds gradually increase the interest rates. They do this when the amount of debt in the economy is growing and they want to bring in more investors to invest in low risk investment types like money market funds and high quality bond funds. What this means to you however, is that the interest rates in the bank increases when this happens. Because of this, the cost of borrowing for you will also increase. As the interest rates increase, the profits of your own business decrease.

The upside of this part of the interest rate cycle is that more people are in the mood for buying houses as the economy begins to recover. In general however, you should avoid borrowing money from banks when the economy is booming because the interest rates tend to be higher.

Another disadvantage of using the banks for financing is their strict screening process. In a nutshell, banks want only to invest in a business that has a good chance of becoming successful. Even if they wanted to, they are usually discouraged by the country's laws and their own policies to lending money to individuals with a history of bad money management.

If you have a questionable credit history, you may get higher interest rates than most people for your loan. You may even be denied the loan altogether if this is the case. The strict process prevents the bank from losing money in case the borrower fails in his or her business and files for bankruptcy.

3. Working with investors

The third option to fund your business project is by going to investors. Generally, this method allows you to pay for the project using other people's money. An investor may either pay a partial amount or the full amount for the house and the renovations. Generally, you will also need to have a profit sharing scheme for each of your projects if you are being funded by an investor.

Generally, you want to be as transparent as possible with your investors from beginning to end. You want to let them know how the money is being spent and how much value each spending adds to the house once it is sold. By being transparent, you are not only

Real Estate Investor

lessening the stress on the end of the investor, you are also building a reputation of being thorough with how you handle your house-flipping projects. This increases the likelihood that your investors will return and invest on your future projects.

There are many types of investors out there. Generally, they are all looking for a vehicle where they can invest their money to achieve a higher yield compared to the investment yields offered by banks and other investment companies. To convince them to invest in your projects, you will need to show that the possible returns for your project will outweigh the risks.

Ideally, you want to find an investor for a joint venture or JV. In a joint venture, the investor only provides the funds and you are in full control of the project. In a case like this, the investor usually does not have the time to actively participate in the project. Instead, they give you the full responsibility of making sure that it is done well and on time. You will still need to report the progress of the project to the investor just to put their mind at ease.

This setup is preferred by most people in the house flipping industry because they do not have a boss to answer to in this system. This allows you to do as you will with the project to increase its market value.

With a JV, the profits are usually split between you and the investor. The percentage of the splitting will depend on the terms agreed upon with the deal. Ideally, you should keep a contract on what was agreed upon on the deal to make sure that there are no misunderstandings in the distribution of the profits.

The second type of investor is called an active investor. This type of investor has the time and the know-how to participate in the business. Because they have the money to fund the project, they usually want to have a say on how the project is being run. You may gain some advantages with this set up if the person investing also has a lot of property management experience to bring to the table. As a beginner, you will have an opportunity to learn if such an investor works with you.

Real Estate Investor

While the investor provides the money, you also bring a lot of important factors to the table. For instance, you provide the manpower and the connections to make the project work. In most cases, this is also an opportunity to make a long term business relationship with someone who has been doing this business for a long period of time.

You may ask, why wouldn't the investor just buy and flip properties for themselves. There may be a variety of reasons for that. One reason may be that they are also involved with other projects that they cannot give 100% of their time on your project. Other investors may also not have knowledge of your area of operations but they also don't want to miss out on a good opportunity to make money.

The disadvantage of working with active investors is that they may interfere with your work. Some of them may disagree with your solutions on how to increase the value of the property. They may also ask for a higher cut of the profits since they are spending time on the project just like you.

4. Peer to peer lending

Peer to peer lending is another good option for gaining capital for your plan. In this process, the lender does not want a cut from the profits. You will need to pay a fixed interest for the project, just like when you are lending from a bank. The big difference is that there will be no strict credit check and your work process will not be affected.

The interest rates for this kind of financing process vary, depending on the person you are borrowing from. If you know the lender personally, you may be able to lower the interest rate, considering that you will not be able to run away from your responsibility of paying off the bill.

Hard Money

Hard money refers to lending institutions outside of banks. These institutions also offer loans to small businesses and personal loans. Just like banks they also do credit checks but they are generally less strict.

5. Alternative payment methods

There multiple other ways for you to pay for the property that you want to work on. One way is by communicating with the seller. In a buyer's market, a seller may be having trouble selling their property. If this is the case, you may provide a solution to taking the property off their plates without shelling out a large of your own pocket. For instance, you can talk with the seller and tell them that you will assume responsibility for paying for the property. This usually works when the seller still has many years' worth or mortgage left on the property.

Chapter 9 – Negotiating for the Property

To negotiate a good deal for the property, you need to work with your broker. The goal in this step of the process is always to get a good price so that you still have room for the renovation expenses.

Do your research about the property

Even if you have decided on the property that you wish to buy, you should stills do more research about it. This time, your reason for doing so is to try to look for factors that will allow you to drive the price lower. Property flipping gurus suggest using the service of property background checkers. These are professionals who keep track of the changes made and services done in properties in a specific area. One example is BuildFax. This organization allows you to check the background of the property so that you will be able to assess its intrinsic value. For a fee, services like these will provide you information like when the pipes of the house were last changed. If you see that some vital parts of the house have not been changed for a while based on your research, you can use this as basis to ask the seller to make the cost lower.

Determine the maximum price you will pay for the house

First, you will need to determine what is the highest you will go for the property. You should make this decision with the post-repairs selling price in mind. You should already have the big picture in your mind or even on paper, regarding the amount your will spend.

To make a good assessment of the maximum price that you will pay for the house, you should consider the asking price and the offers already made for it. If you are projecting that you will be able to sell the property for $230,000 for example, your total cost should be $130,000 to make a profit of a hundred grand. If you can get the property for $130,000 and set a $50,000 budget for the fixes, you should still get $50,000 in profit. Any more spending will be deducted from your projected profits.

Make an offer

From the amount above, the next step is to identify your first offer price. When you visit, the broker of the seller should be able to tell you of the asking price of the property. You should also ask if an offer has already been made above the asking price. You will know if you will be able to get this property within the budget based on the other offers.

The properties perfect for remodeling often, does not get a lot of attention. You will only get to compete for the price if there are other house-flipping teams in the area. Even so, they are not likely to compete with you. The last thing a house flipping businessperson wants is a price war.

When making your offer, you should always keep the price low. If the total amount that you are willing to pay is lower than the asking price, you should offer 10% to 30% below your maximum budget for the house.

Ideally, you want to be the one with the first offer for a property that is meant to be renovated. If other people planning the same thing see that you already made an offer, they may choose to move on to another property to avoid a price war.

You should not use the same mentality when making your offers. Even if you see that others already made offers in the property, you should still give your offer as long as it is within your budget for the property. Because house hunters generally do not want a price war, they may give you the property. Only when the offer is topped should you stop pushing your luck and look for a house with less competition.

Anticipate the counter-offer

Real Estate Investor

The point of making in offer is for both parties to negotiate and reach an agreement for a price that they can both live with. In most cases, the final price for the property end up to be the middle ground between the asking price and the first offer made by the buyer. You will have to consider this every time you make an offer.

To make an offer for the property, you will need to communicate the amount to your broker. In a real estate deal, it is usually only the brokers who communicate. You could also do the negotiating if you want to take on this task.

When negotiating for a lower price, make sure that the seller (or the broker), knows why you think the property should be valued less than the asking price. The primary reason that you should cite is the fixes that need to be made on the property. These fixes will require extra expenses on your part and you will need to keep the buying price low.

It is not advisable to tell the sellers that you are buying the property to flip it. When sellers hear this, they usually think about the profits that you are about to make. Most sellers react to this by mentioning the profits that you are about to make from the property. Being a beginner in the business gives you the luxury to hide your intentions just yet. You may need to say your intentions for the property if it does come up. If it does not come up though, there is no need to mention it proactively.

After you give the initial offer, you should expect the seller to give you a lower asking price if they are serious in making a deal. When they do give you a counter for the first offer you made, this usually means that they are willing to give up their position to make the deal work. Your next step will depend on your buying philosophy.

The first option is to buy the property if it is already below the maximum amount that you are willing to pay for the property. This option will not get you all the properties you need at the lowest price. What it will do however, is it will give you a good reputation among local brokers.

Brokers usually get paid on commission based on the total selling price of the properties. If you don't haggle too much, you may build a good image with them so that they will give you tips in future properties that they are handling. This will make the process of buying homes easier for you in the future.

The second option is to keep haggling even when the asking price is already below your limit. This option is dangerous because it may cause the seller to pull out of the negotiation and look for some other buyers. The advantage of having this kind of buying philosophy is that you will be able to get all the properties at the lowest possible price.

There is only one rule for negotiating for the price; don't make a deal for properties priced over your budget. If the seller will not budge, you should be willing to walk away from a property. If you cannot get the property below your budget for it, you will not be able to make money from it.

Closing the deal

When you have agreed on a price with the seller, the next step is to finalize the deal and to finish the paperwork needed. Your broker will be the one to arrange all these. Just make sure though, to read the documents especially in your first few purchases. Even though your broker is the one handling this side of the business, you still want to be familiar with all the documents that you need to sign.

Chapter 10 – Getting Things Fixed

Now that you have the property, you should decide on the parts that you want to fix, remove or upgrade.

- Delegate almost all tasks

When working on flipping a house, you do not need to worry about doing all the tasks yourself. Most shows about flipping houses on TV show the host doing a lot of the manual labor. In reality though, this is not the case. Most parts of the job are done by the crew of the contractor. If you and your team want to participate in the painting or in adding wallpaper, you are free to do so. However, you should remember that many of the tasks in fixing a house up require specialized skills. Adding tiles to the floor may seem easy but in reality, special techniques are required to make sure that there are no air bubbles between the tiles and the cement. It also takes an experienced hand to line the tiles up so that they look like they were done by a professional.

In general, your job is to find the right people to do the project for you. You do not need to learn new skills or do things by trial and error.

- Look for a theme that will fit the taste of your target market

The most common challenge of flipping a house is the task of turning an outdated house design to something stylish and modern. The best design for the house will depend on the type of market you are catering to. However, it will be much easier for you to make a design work by thinking of a theme for the project.

When thinking of improving the appearance of the house, you should think of a theme to organize your design ideas. If you just got a property overlooking the ocean for example, you may design a Mediterranean theme with white as the primary color and complimented by blue and one more earth color.

The simple trick of putting a theme on your design will make it easier for you to create a design that looks modern and elegant at the same time.

- Improve the overall look of the house

In most cases, you will need to fix the parts of the home that gives it its overall look. These include the exterior paint job and the roofing. All signs of wear and tear and weathering should be removed, replaced or fixed. Most buyers are particular about cracks and water damage, so you should keep an eye for those as well. The exterior of the home should be absolutely stunning if you want to invite people to check it out.

You should also take note of the fixes necessary in the entrance of the home. The entrance gives your future buyers their first impression of the property. The majority of buyers make the decision if they like a property in the first 15 minutes of seeing and entering it. Because of this, you should make sure that you the entrance to the property has no negative features.

When first entering the property, take note of the steps towards the entrance. Ask yourself if it has the tendency to puddle when it rains or will it be slippery when wet. From the entrance, look at the front face of the property and look for flaws. In particular, try to spot damages and unsightly parts. If the plants in the front of the home do not work well with the paint, change either or even both of them. Watch out for broken windows and rusted metal parts.

After the entrance, your buyers will next experience the living areas of the house. At this point, you should pay attention to the small details that give the property its overall look. This includes the wall paper, the flooring, the entry of light and the fixtures.

The wallpaper or the paint for the wall will determine the vibe of each room. Different shades of white will make the room more spacious that it actually is. If house requires wallpapers, make sure to change old-fashioned designs with the modern patterns we have now, as they fit the theme.

- Focus on the basics first

Before you go into installing new things in the house, focus your efforts and your budget first on the basic things. Have all the lighting and electrical fixtures fixed first. Check the entire house for leaks. This includes leaks in the pipes as well as in the roof. If you see any part that is leaking, you should also check if there is water damage right below it.

Aside from this, you should also look into the basic safety features of the house. Check if it has fire alarms installed or of the gas pipes entering the house have been updated. It is common for the previous owners of the house to neglect these aspects.

You may also need to modernize some parts of the house including the wiring, and air conditioning and heating systems. In general, you want to make sure that the house is ready for occupancy.

All these details should be dealt with first because some types of fixes tend to be costly. If you avoid fixes until the end of the project, you may be surprised with the big expenses that may lead you to go over the budget.

Only when all the basic fixes are done should you go on to add value adding features.

- Making the kitchen modern

In most homes that require renovations, the kitchen is usually the part that needs it most. In old homes, this part usually shows the most signs of wear and tear. The appliances may look old or worn because of use. The materials in the counter may look old and some may even be damaged. Because of the amount of activity done in the kitchen, it is usually the least maintained part of the house.

For fixing up the kitchen, you want to make it look modern. It should also go with the overall design of the house that you are looking for.

The counters and the cupboards dominate the overall look of the kitchen along with the large appliances like the refrigerator and the stove or oven. If these appliances are already modern you may keep them. However, if their design looks like they were bought in the 90s, you may have trouble selling it to future buyers.

As for the counters, you will need to make sure that they don't look moldy or damaged. Sometimes, this means replacing the surface altogether.

The kitchen is an important part of the house because it is one of the places where the adults of the house spend most of their time. Many home buyers consider the kitchen as one of the most important parts to consider when buying a permanent home.

- Make the bathrooms bright and easy to clean

The bathrooms are probably the second dealmaker in a house. If the bathrooms are bright, they give an illusion of space to the buyer. This will make the home easier to sell. When making changes in the bathrooms, try to add windows in strategic places in the wall where natural light can enter. Also choose white as the dominant color. You may add one other color in your design for accent but keep most of the surfaces white.

- Avoid luxury upgrades

Most people starting out in the house flipping business think that adding luxury items will increase the value of the property. In reality, most luxury items will only add to the cost of your property and not to the after-repair price of the property. The classic example is the swimming pool. Swimming pools are great for exercising and for entertaining guests. However, they can also be costly to maintain. In most cases, families with small children will avoid properties with pools. By adding a pool to a property with a big backyard, you only increase the expenses without adding much value to the house.

Real Estate Investor

The only exception to this is when a pool is a need in the area rather than a luxury. In areas like New Mexico for example, many people want to have a pool at home for the hot summers.

- Focus on people's needs instead

Instead of adding rooms and accessories that you think your buyers will like, you should instead focus on the needs of the market. When looking for inspiration on upgrades that you can do for the new property, you may take the time to visit the properties listed in the market. In particular, you should look for properties that are popular with buyers. These types of properties do not usually stay long in the market.

When checking them out, you should look at its qualities that make it stand out in the market. In particular, you should look at its basic features like the number of rooms and baths. You should also look at the natural lighting features as well as the colors used for the wallpapers or the paint for the room.

You should take a mental note of the positive qualities that that popular properties in your market have that can be applied to the home that you are working on. Some of the things you can do. If the house that you are working on still has space in the yard, you may add another room to it. This type of renovation will cost you a lot. However, if this upgrade will add a serious bump in the price of the property (based on the prices of properties in the market), you should consider doing it.

Aside from looking at the available houses in the area, you may also have the house you are about to flip listed at a higher price or you could have a private showing to a group of buyers that your broker can gather for you. You may set the price higher to make sure that it will not be bought. After showing it off, you should ask the buyers, what additional features they want from the house. Most of them will be happy to discuss possible improvements that could be made for the property.

After discussing the changes needed, you may also ask them if they would be interested in the house if you made the renovations they requested. While most buyers would have already found a house by then, their insights on how to improve the property may be helpful.

- Make the lawn presentable

It is common for house remodeling professionals to neglect the lawn and the other exterior parts of the house. While these parts have no added value to the buyer other than aesthetics, it still occupies a large part of the appearance of the house. If the house has a grass lawn, make sure that it is mowed before selling it and that all the patches are covered. Also add plants that may cover unsightly areas and enhance the colors of the house. Studies suggest that houses with greens in the outside sell faster than their purely cement counterparts.

Chapter 11 – Selling the Property

All the activities you've done so far culminate to the selling of the house. If you cannot sell the house at the right price, the entire project is a failure. To make sure that you sell the property fast, you need to follow the steps in this chapter:

- Sit down with your broker and set up a solid marketing plan

Most people sell houses like they would sell their other items in the house. This, however is an ineffective way of selling properties because people usually consider houses as long-term investments. The buying process for houses is much more different compared to other high ticket items. You will need to make a person commit to a product for 20-30 years when selling a house.

Instead of listing the house on Craigslist, you should have a solid marketing plan drawn up to make sure that you reach the right number of people who fit the profile of your target market.

Even before the renovation is done, you should already sit down with your broker to discuss your strategy on how you will sell the house. You need to do this so that you will be able to find out what your broker will do on his end to hasten the selling process.

This will allow you to gauge the level of commitment that your broker has on the process. Most brokers handle multiple properties at a time to increase their chances of earning. This may also mean however, that they will have lesser time for each property that they are handling. While you cannot force your broker to do more for your property, you can do your own marketing strategies.

Real Estate Investor

- Start marketing your business

When you market your business, do not just advertise the specific house that you are selling. People who see ads of specific houses often forget them. Instead, have a brand name under which you will market your business. It will be more profitable for you in the long run to do it using this approach.

To market the properties in your inventory, you should have multiple places where you will have them listed. A website is one of the first marketing assets that you should get. Have a professional create a website for you sporting your business name as its domain name.

You should specify that the website should show the properties that you have listed for sale with a part showing photos the newly renovated property. It is important that you show the price and each of the rooms and living areas. The website should serve as a place where the prospective buyers can tour the house without actually going to the property. This will allow you to market the property to people outside of the local area.

Aside from the photos, you could also have a video tour of the house. You or your broker can show off the house to the camera just like when you are selling it to a real person. This will allow people from other cities or even states to look at the property.

Aside from having a website made, you should also consider having the property listed with your broker's website and firm. Brokers usually have a list of people they can pitch your property to. They are usually well connected in the market and are also the go to people of local property buyers. By connecting with one, you will be able to sell your properties much faster compared to doing the selling on your own.

In particular, you are looking to leverage their connections outside of your local area. Most brokers have connections with other brokers in other cities. When people they know move, they are able to use these connections to cater to the needs of their moving clients.

Aside from what your broker does, you should also list down the things that you will do on your end to sell the property faster. You should already start listing the names of the people you know who may be interested in the house or who may know someone who will be.

- Look for other online tools

You will also find a lot of other online tools where you can have your properties listed. For instance, you can sign up to various online real estate listing websites. You could also advertise using Google AdWords to show your listings to people who are looking for houses in your area using the search engine. While the online real estate market is extremely competitive, you may be able to lessen the cost and trim down the competition by limiting your ads to people who are looking for homes in your specific area.

- Showing the house

When showing photos of the properties, it may be advantageous to show the property fully furnished. You should specify that these furnishings are not included in the sale.

When marketing the house in photos and videos, make sure to add models of your target market in them. If you are planning to sell the house in to families for instance, you can host a party with friends and family members to make them models of your new property. You could also hire models to fill in the space for you.

By putting people in your marketing materials, you will be able to help the prospective buyers visualize what it is like living in the house. They will be able to imagine how it will be like when they are the ones living in the property.

When showing off the house, you should highlight the positive qualities of the house while having a good answer when buyers bring up the negative parts. You should make sure to lessen the impact of the negative comments of the property.

- Build your connections

Connections will help you sell properties fast. When people see that you are in the house selling business, you will be the first person in their minds when someone asks them for properties being sold in the area.

To start letting people know that you are in this business, you should begin by creating an elevator pitch of what you do. An elevator pitch is a short line that you should use when people ask you want you do for a living. Most would just say that they are in the real estate remodeling business or that they flip houses. They then move on with the conversation after that.

Instead of doing this, you should elaborate your pitch to two or three sentences. For instance, you can add the area where you operate and the number of houses you have in your inventory right now. Lastly, you could tell the people you are talking with to give you a call if they are in the market for a new home or if they know someone who is.

After creating your elevator pitch, you should consider increasing the frequency you go out in social events. This will allow you to widen your circles. In particular, you should go to real estate related events where you will meet a lot of other brokers. Brokers, for example, host parties and get together when they are showing another property to the market. You can go to one of these parties, not to sell your own property but to meet other brokers that you may call in the future when you have new properties to sell.

If you are the outgoing type, you may also host one of these parties to increase visibility of your home.

- Start showing commitment to your business

You should also start marketing yourself as someone committed to real estate renovations. If you are planning to keep buying and

Real Estate Investor

flipping properties in the long run, you should consider getting real estate brokerage license in your state. This will allow you to sell properties in your area without the need for a broker to process the deals for you.

Chapter 12 – Earning 6-figures from Your Real Estate Business

Each sale in the house flipping business will give you a net profit of tens of thousands of dollars even if you are flipping for an investor. In this chapter, we will discuss the various ways on how you can manage your business so that you will get a six-figure income each month.

Increase your property inventory

To increase your income, you should consider taking in more properties to increase your chances of making a sale. Having multiple properties in your inventory will require you to take in more risk. However it will also increase your earning potential each year.

To take in more properties, you should start by increasing saving a higher percentage of your profits from your previous deals. This will allow you to increase your emergency fund and your working capital. This will require sacrifices on your part. Not everyone has the discipline for delayed gratification. However, if you want to boost the income potential of your house flipping business, you should develop this discipline.

Aside from saving your own money, you should also consider taking in more investors. Having more investors will allow you to take in more individual projects. When doing this, you should let the investor know that the partnership will be on a per-project basis. If you already have a company set up, they are not particularly investing in the company itself but in the project the company is working on.

Widen your area of operation

To increase the number of houses in your inventory, you may also need to widen your area of operation. If you only operated in one side of the city in the past, you may want to consider buying properties in the other side of town now. You will need to do this because the number of people selling properties at prices below the market value will also increase if you widen your area of operation.

This does pose some challenges though. One of the biggest challenges will be logistics. You will need to find another source of materials for your renovation if your current source is too far away. You should also consider the travel time for the crew who will be working with you on your other projects. Will they be able to meet you on the site of the construction or do you need to provide transportation provisions for them?

You should also consider your own travel options. If you are working on two or more projects across the city, you will need to manage your time wisely. The travel time between projects will take a lot of hours from your day. Ideally, you should communicate with your point persons in each project via phone and just check on them every other day. This will only work if you trust the people you are working with.

Finding more people

By taking on more properties, you may also find it more challenging to find more people to work on the project. Most of the people you will be hiring will be contractors. Getting more of them to sign up can be a challenge especially if your renovations require special trade skills.

To manage this part of the business, you will need to communicate with more than one contractors. Because these are project based hires, you will be paying more per day for their services but you will also spend less in the long run compared to hiring full time employees.

Increase your insurance coverage

Aside from the factors mentioned above, you should also increase the premium and the coverage of your property insurance. This will ensure that you are protected for unforeseen events like natural calamities. These type of events has the potential of damaging multiple of your real estate investments. You can protect your assets by making sure that they are covered in cases of accidents.

Keep your credit score in good condition

As stated in earlier chapters, you will need to make loans to fund most of these house flipping projects. If you want to maximize your income from this business, you need to keep your credit score in good condition. This will allow you to keep making loans with low interest rates, thereby increasing your profit per project. The lesser you need to pay off the banks, the higher your income will be for each project.

Aim to improve efficiency

After setting things up to increase your inventory size, the next step is to make the entire process even more efficient. The goal in this step is to decrease the time between buying and selling the properties in your inventory. You should do this while keeping the cost of the business low.

To improve your business efficiency, you will need to work with the people working on each project. A contractor for instance usually sets a date when the project will be finished. This is part of the basis for the amount that you pay each contractor. However, there are times when the project takes longer than expected to be done. This can happen for a number of reasons and is not always the contractor's fault. However, if your contractor is unable to keep to the deadline most of the time, you should consider changing contractors to the ones who can work within their given schedules.

You should also consider the source of the materials used for construction and renovation. While most people would just go to the local hardware warehouse, you may be able to decrease the cost without compromising the quality by communicating directly with the companies that make these materials. If you are need a lot of cement every month for your business, why not try to get a good deal with the cement factory directly? This will decrease the cost per sack of cement that you buy. You need to apply this principle to all of the products that you use regularly in your home renovations to lessen the overall cost of each project.

Lastly, you should also increase the efficiency of your sales process. If your broker is not doing well in selling your properties, you should consider changing brokers. It is also highly advisable to hire a company real estate broker if your inventory of houses is growing. This way, all sales communications will be handled by just one person. You will also be able to focus more on the buying part of the business where in you make sure that you can get great quality properties for low prices.

Move to higher end properties

If you have built enough funds to work on bigger houses, you should certainly do so. While there are fewer people who can afford bigger properties, most of them do not have limitations in budget. You may be able to do more creatively and add more value to the homes you flip. You will also need a wider connection base of people in real estate business to start selling to the high end housing markets. This may mean that you need to build your reputation first as a fixer-upper of houses. If you can build a reputation that your renovations are of high quality, you may be able to transition well to this market.

Conclusion

Thank you again for downloading this book!

I hope this book was able to help you to plan your entry strategy into the business of flipping houses.

The next step is to do your own feasibility study of implementing the strategies in this book to your own location.

This business may seem scary at first. However, as you improve your connections and skills, the business will become significantly easier for you. With experience, it will be faster for you to find houses to flip. You will also learn the best types of fixes for each home to increase the value of the home. Most importantly, it will be faster for you to sell houses because of the connections you've built from past deals. The more you experience you gain in this field, the better you become at it. It's time for you to start you first deal.

Thank you and good luck!

www.ingramcontent.com/pod-product-compliance
Lightning Source LLC
Chambersburg PA
CBHW050022230526
45470CB00003B/1086